A Visit to a Space Station

Claire Throp

Raintree is an imprint of Capstone Global Library Limited, a company incorporated in England and Wales having its registered office at 7 Pilgrim Street, London, EC4V 6LB – Registered company number: 6695582

www.raintreepublishers.co.uk
myorders@raintreepublishers.co.uk

Text © Capstone Global Library Limited 2014
First published in hardback in 2014
Paperback edition first published in 2015
The moral rights of the proprietor have been asserted.

Edited by Dan Nunn and Catherine Veitch
Designed by Cynthia Akiyoshi
Picture research by Ruth Blair
Production by Vicki Fitzgerald
Originated by Capstone Global Library Limited
Printed and bound in China

ISBN 978 1 406 27181 2 (hardback)
17 16 15 14 13
10 9 8 7 6 5 4 3 2 1

ISBN 978 1 406 27186 7 (paperback)
18 17 16 15
10 9 8 7 6 5 4 3 2 1

British Library Cataloguing in Publication Data
A full catalogue record for this book is available from the British Library.

Acknowledgements
We would like to thank the following for permission to reproduce photographs: Corbis p. 19 (© NASA/Reuters); ESA pp. 11, 21, 23, 25, 26, 28; Gagarin Cosmonaut Training Centre p. 6; Getty Images pp. 8 (Sergei Remezov/AFP), 9 (Bill Ingalls/NASA); NASA pp. 12, 14, 15, 16, 18; Science Photo Library pp. 13, 24 (NASA), 20 (CHASSENET/BSIP); Superstock pp. 4 and title page (Science and Society), 5 rocket, 17 (Ben Cooper/Science Faction), 5 child (Blend Images), 7 (StockTrek Images/Purestock), 10, 22, 25 (StockTrek Images), 27 (dieKleinert), 29 (Science Photo Library).

Cover photograph of an astronaut reproduced with permission of Shutterstock (© iurii).

Every effort has been made to contact copyright holders of material reproduced in this book. Any omissions will be rectified in subsequent printings if notice is given to the publisher.

Some words are shown in bold, **like this**. You can find out what they mean by looking in the glossary.

Contents

Let's take a trip to a
space station 4

Be prepared 6

Lift off! 8

Arrival 10

Everyday life 12

Supplies 16

Free time 18

Exercise 20

Work 22

Science in space 26

Back to Earth 28

Glossary 30

Find out more 31

Index 32

Let's take a trip to a space station

Space stations stay in space for many years. People go there to live and work for four to six months. Let's take a trip to the **International Space Station (ISS)**. Put on your spacesuit and get ready to blast off.

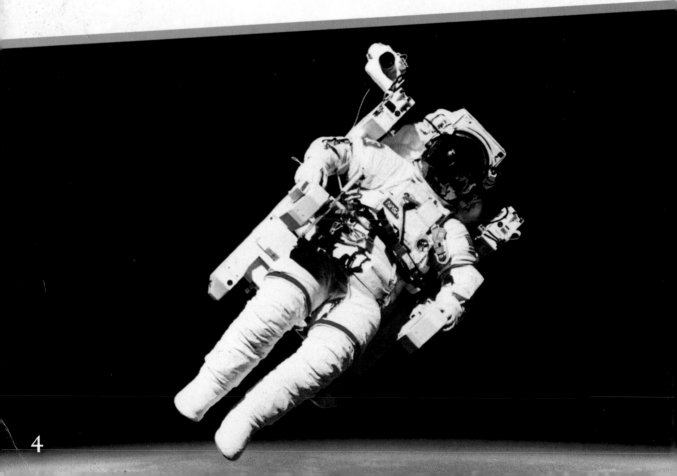

Be prepared

Gravity is the force that holds us to the ground when we are on Earth. There is very little gravity on a **space station**. This means that if something – or someone – is not tied down, it floats away. You'll need to do some hard training before we go.

Moving in water is a good way to train for walking in space.

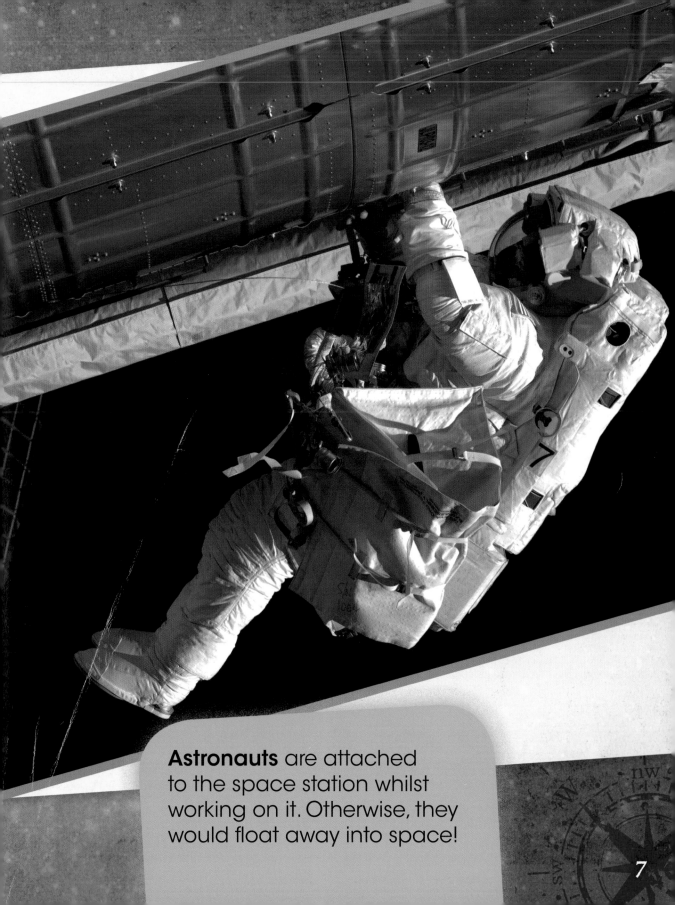

Astronauts are attached
to the space station whilst
working on it. Otherwise, they
would float away into space!

Lift off!

To get to the **space station**, we have to travel in a Russian *Soyuz* spacecraft. **Astronauts** strap themselves into special seats because there is very little room to move around.

Make sure you are comfortable because this journey will take 2 days!

Did you know?

The journey to the space station takes longer than the return to Earth. This is because it takes a while for any spaceship to catch up with the moving space station.

Arrival

We have arrived! Our spacecraft links with the **space station** at a **docking port**. Once the spacecraft is locked on, doors called hatches open to allow us into the space station.

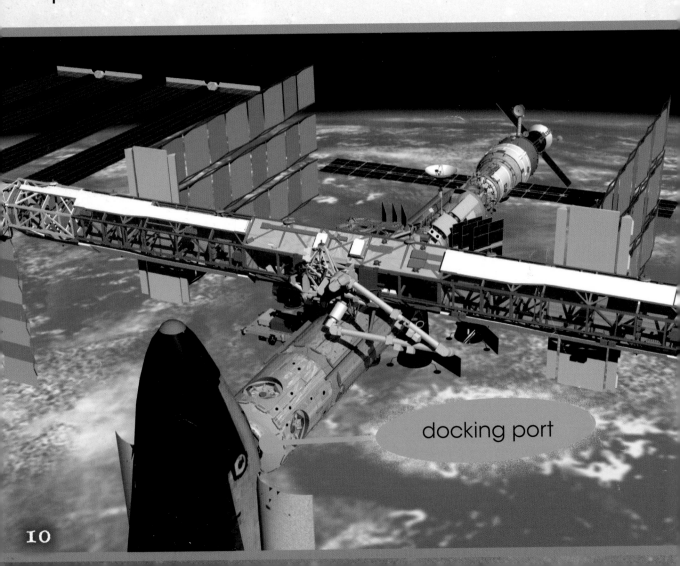

docking port

This part of the space station is called Zarya.

Everyday life

Astronauts sleep in sleep stations about the size of a large fridge. Astronauts cannot have showers because the water would float away. Many astronauts use wipes and dry shampoo instead.

Did you know?

Astronauts sneeze about 100 times a day! This is because dust does not settle on a surface as it does in our homes. It floats in the air.

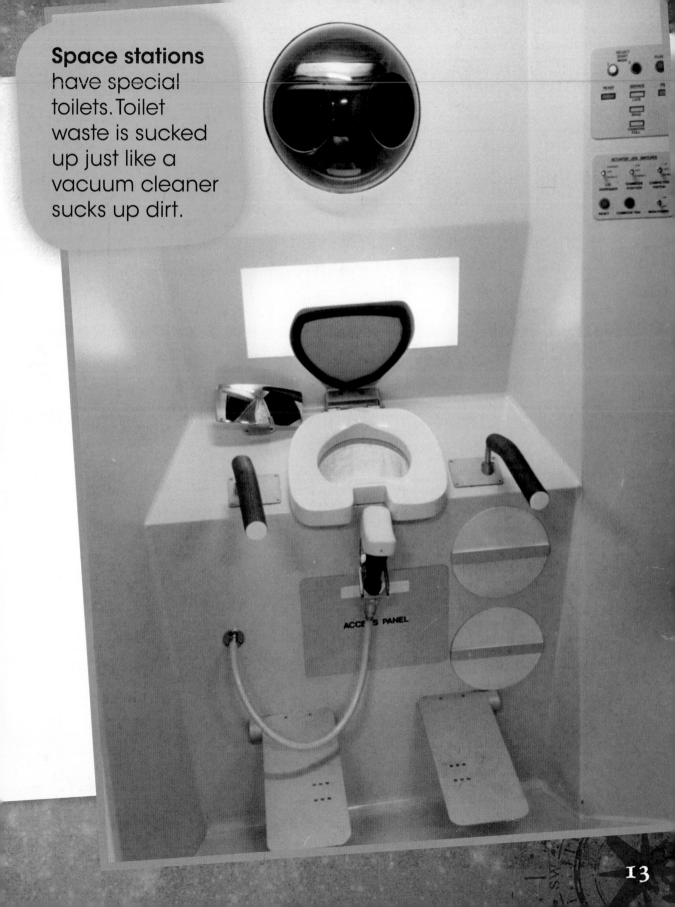

Space stations have special toilets. Toilet waste is sucked up just like a vacuum cleaner sucks up dirt.

ACCESS PANEL

13

It's dinner time! The food on a **space station** is **dehydrated**. This means it has had water removed so that it can stay fresh longer. **Astronauts** add water to the food so they can eat it.

Other food on space stations is in packages that just need to be heated up.

Did you know?

Some astronauts eat with trays of food strapped to their legs! If it wasn't attached to them, the food would float away.

Supplies

The **European Space Agency's (ESA)** Automated Transfer Vehicle (ATV) is used to take **supplies** to the **space station** about once a year. This includes fuel, equipment and food.

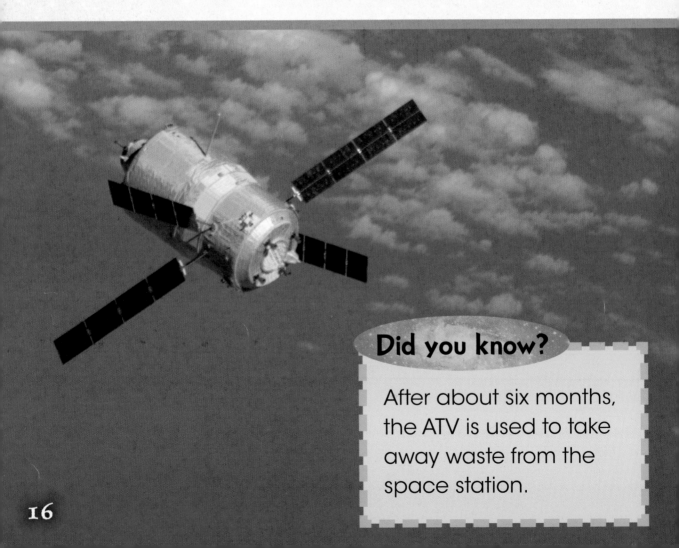

Did you know?

After about six months, the ATV is used to take away waste from the space station.

Supplies are kept in spaces under the floor and in the walls.

Free time

Astronauts on a **space station** have time off from work, just like we do on Earth. Some play musical instruments. Others may play games or watch films. They also all get time to talk to their family or friends back on Earth.

The **cupola** is an area where astronauts can see Earth through a large window.

Exercise

Astronauts have to exercise on a **space station** to keep their muscles healthy. Because there is very little **gravity**, astronauts don't use their legs much. Their leg and back muscles become weak.

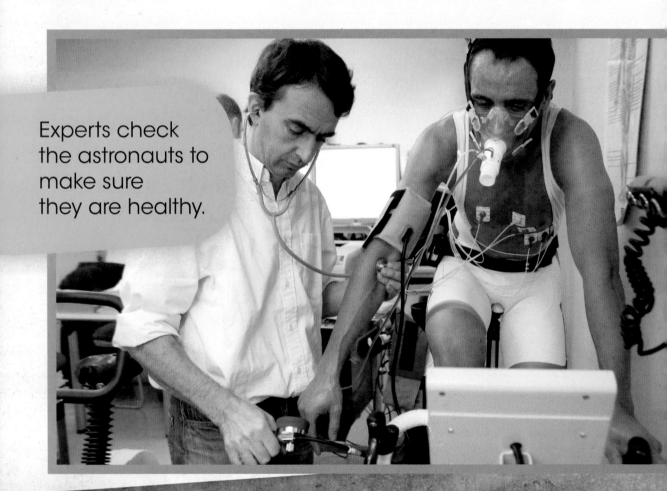

Experts check the astronauts to make sure they are healthy.

Did you know?

Astronauts on the **ISS** exercise for about two hours every day.

Work

To keep the **space station** in good working order, repairs and checks need to be carried out. **Astronauts** working on the outside are attached to the station by a safety line called a **tether**.

tether

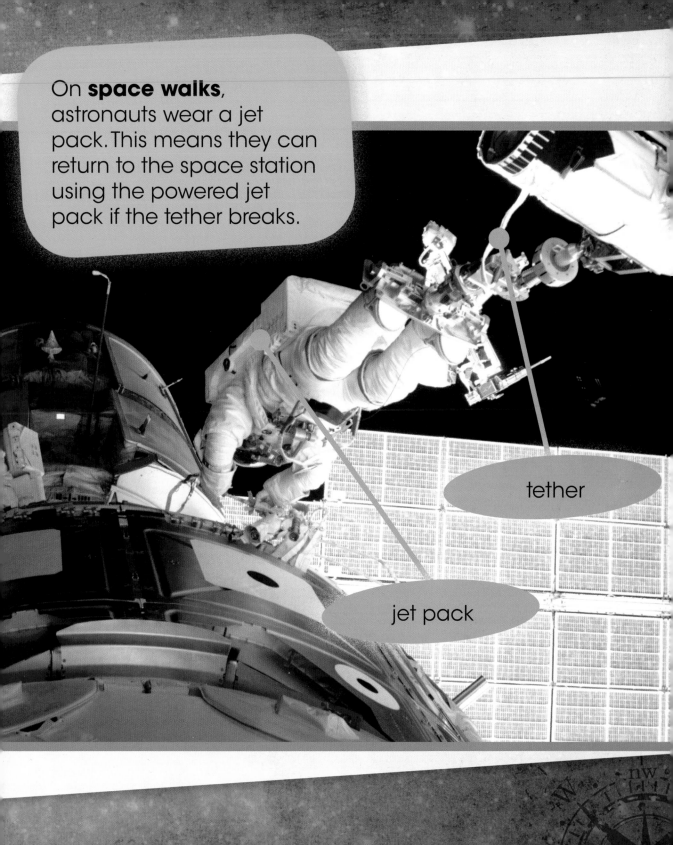

On **space walks**, astronauts wear a jet pack. This means they can return to the space station using the powered jet pack if the tether breaks.

tether

jet pack

Some **astronauts** have the job of taking photographs of the **space station**, Earth, the Sun and space. This can be done from inside the space station or outside.

Did you know?

The **ISS** is more than 300 kilometres above Earth. That is about the same distance as Birmingham to Dublin.

photograph of the space station taken by an astronaut

Science in space

Scientists carry out experiments in **laboratories** on board the **ISS**. They test different materials such as metal and liquids to see how they behave in space. Scientists also see how living in space affects people's bodies.

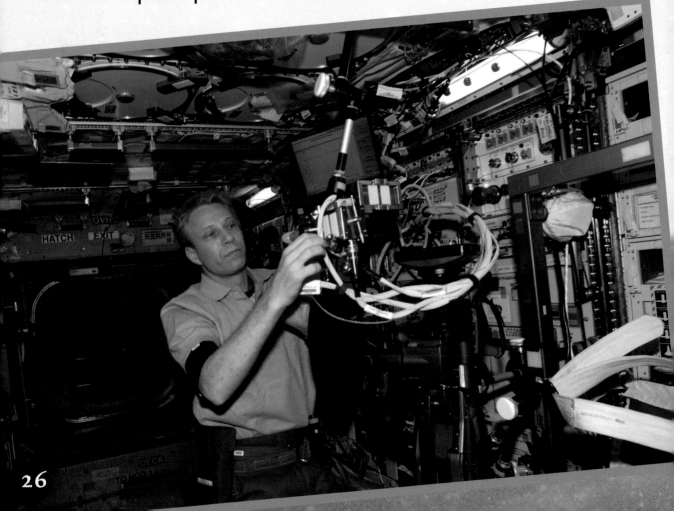

This is Columbus, a science laboratory on board the ISS.

Back to Earth

It is time to blast back down to Earth. Returning to Earth after six months can be tough. Some **astronauts** have trouble standing up because it can take a while to adjust.

Did you know?

Several countries have worked together to build the **ISS**. It has taken many missions to take all the parts out and fix them together in space.

Glossary

astronaut someone who is specially trained to work in space

cupola area on the ISS where astronauts can see Earth through a large window

dehydrated dried from having water removed

docking port place where a spacecraft joins with a space station by locking onto it

European Space Agency (ESA) organization that runs the European space programme

gravity force that attracts things to the centre of Earth

International Space Station (ISS) space station built by a number of different countries

laboratory room where scientific tests can be carried out

space station large structure that stays in space for a long time. People can live and work there.

space walk time an astronaut spends outside a space station in space

supplies stock or store of something such as food

tether safety line that attaches the astronaut to the space station when they are working outside it

Find out more

Books

First Encyclopedia of Space, Paul Dowswell
(Usborne, 2010)

In Space (Machines Rule), Steve Parker
(Franklin Watts, 2011)

Space (Explorer Tales), Nick Hunter (Raintree, 2013)

The Best Book of Spaceships, Ian Graham
(Kingfisher, 2008)

Websites

www.esa.int/esaKIDSen/SpaceStations.html
Learn more about space stations on the European
Space Agency's website.

www.nasa.gov/audience/forkids/home/index.html
Find out about the ISS and other information about
space on NASA's website.

**www.nasa.gov/mission_pages/station/main/suni_
iss_tour.html**
This NASA web page has several videos that give
tours around different parts of the ISS.

Index

astronauts 7, 8, 12, 14, 15, 18–24, 28, 30
Automated Transfer Vehicle (ATV) 16

Columbus 27
cupola 19, 30

dehydrated 14, 30
docking ports 10, 30
dust 12

European Space Agency (ESA) 16, 30
exercise 20–21

food 14, 15, 16
free time 18
fuel 16

gravity 6, 20, 30

hatches 10

International Space Station (ISS) 4, 10–29, 30

jet packs 23

laboratories 26, 27, 30

photographs 24, 25

repairs 22

scientific experiments 26–27
sleep stations 12
sneezing 12
Soyuz spacecraft 8
space walks 6, 23, 30
spacecraft 8, 9, 10
supplies 16–17, 30

tethers 22, 23, 30
toilets 13
training 6

washing 12
waste 13, 16

Zarya 11